Handy Kentucky Genealogy Handbook

By

Gary L.Morris

©2015 Gary L. Morris

ISBN-13: 978-1506147772

ISBN-10: 1506147771

Table of Contents

NOTES

About Genealogical Research in Kentucky

Tracing your family history in Kentucky can be a fascinating trip through time. Kentucky was home to iconic of American figures such as Henry Clay and Daniel Boone. Locating the relevant genealogical records you'll need to find your ancestors however can be a frustrating experience. To help you avoid those frustrations when tracing your Kentucky ancestry, we'll show you which records you'll need, and help you to understand:

1. What they are
2. Where to find them
3. How to use them

These records can be found both online and off, so we'll introduce you to online websites, indexes and databases, as well as brick-and-mortar repositories and other institutions that will help with your research in Kentucky. So that you will have a more comprehensive understanding of these records, we have provided a brief history of the "Bluegrass State" to illustrate what type of records may have been generated during specific time periods. That information will assist you in pinpointing times and locations on which to focus the search for your Kentucky ancestors and their records.

A Brief History of Kentucky

Kentucky was quite inaccessible to settlement during the colonization era due to the rugged mountain terrain that separated it from the coastal colonies. France first claimed the area in the early 18th century which caused British interest in the region to be heightened. Hunters and explorers scouted the eastern mountain region during this time, but settlement was delayed by the French and Indian Wars between 1754 and 1763. After the British proved victorious, settlers began to migrate to the area, albeit against a British proclamation forbidding any settlements west of the Appalachian Mountains.

One of the first of these early settlers was Daniel Boone, who helped to blaze the Wilderness road which stretched from Tennessee into the Kentucky area, and established one of the first settlements known as Boonesboro. The legality of the settlement at Boonesbor was challenged by Virginia who laid claim to the area. Kentucky became a county of Virginia in 1776, and settlers from there began journeying to the area. The early Virginian settlers had many conflicts with the Native American populace, though their resistance was ended at the Battle of Fallen Timbers in 1794.

Kentucky was admitted to the Union in 1792, and as it entered the 19th century, it remained a state of small plantations and farms. Slave labour was not popular in Kentucky, and the importation of slaves into the state was banned in 1833. That law was repealed in 1850 however, and Kentucky soon became a major slave market for the lower South. Emancipationists fought against the new law and consequently by the outbreak of the Civil War, Kentucky was divided by this conflict.

Kentucky attempted to remain neutral at the outbreak of the Civil War, and the state refused to sanction Abraham Lincoln's call for volunteers. Confederate forces entered Kentucky and occupied areas in the south, including Bowling Green and Columbus. The state voted to oust the Confederates in September, 1861, and General Grant invaded and took Paducah, securing the state's Union status.

The effects of the Civil War were felt nowhere as strongly in Kentucky, where neighbors, friends, and families became bitterly divided. More than 60,000 troops from Kentucky fought for the Union, approximately 30,000 for the Confederate forces. Many opposed the Reconstruction policies after the war, and ratification of the thirteenth and fourteenth amendments were refused by the State.

Following the war commercial and industrial recovery was fueled by the construction of railroads, though Kentucky remained a one crop agricultural state – tobacco. The price of tobacco plummeted after the Civil War, and buyers and growers clashed sparking what was known as the Black Patch War. Night riders from both sides terrorized each other, and general lawlessness prevailed for more than a year until a truce was forced by the state militia in 1908.

Important Dates in Kentucky History

- **1750** - Thomas Walker explores Kentucky through the Cumberland Gap
- **1751** - Christopher Gist explores area along Ohio River.
- **1763** - France cedes area including Kentucky to Britain.
- **1775** - Boiling Springs and St. Asaph settled.
- **1782** - "Last battle of American Revolution" fought at Blue Licks, near Mount Olivet.
- **1792** - Kentucky becomes the 15th state on June 1, 1792.
- **1796** - Wilderness Road opened to wagons.
- **1798** - Legislature passes Kentucky Resolutions opposing United States Alien and Sedition Acts.
- **1812** - Kentuckians bear brunt of war with England north of the Ohio and in New Orleans.
- **1818** - Westernmost region of the state was annexed, following its purchase from the Chicasaw Indians.
- **1819** - The first commercial oil well was on the Cumberland River in McCreary County Kentucky in 1819.
- **1830** - Louisville and Portland Canal opened.
- **1861** - Kentucky declares its neutrality in American Civil War.
- **1862** - The first major battle on Kentucky soil during the Civil War was fought near Prestonsburg, January 10, 1862, bloodiest Civil War Battle to be fought on Kentucky soil was the Battle of Perryville, Oct. 8, 1862.

Famous Battles Fought in Kentucky

Civil War battles were fought at Richmond, Mills Springs, and Perryville in 1862, but after that there were no major battles in Kentucky. Below you fill find a list of the major battles that took place on Kentucky soil along with links to websites where you can learn more about them.

These battle accounts can be very effective in uncovering the military records of your ancestor. They can tell you what regiments fought in which battles, and often include the names and ranks of many officers and enlisted men.

Battle of Blue Licks, 1782 – American Revolutionary War

Battle of Blue Licks, 1782:
http://www.battleofbluelicks.org/html/history.html

Battle of Perryville, 1862 – Civil War

Battle of Perryville, 1862: http://www.battleofperryville.com/

Battle of Mill Springs, 1862 – Civil War

Battle of Mill Springs, 1862:
http://www.civilwar.org/battlefields/mill-springs.html

Battle of Richmond, 1862 – Civil War

Battle of Richmond, 1862:
http://www.nps.gov/hps/abpp/battles/ky007.htm

Common Kentucky Genealogical Issues and Resources to Overcome Them

Boundary Changes: Boundary changes are a common obstacle when researching Kentucky ancestors. You could be searching for an ancestor's record in one county when in fact it is stored in a different one due to historical county boundary changes. The **Atlas of Historical County Boundaries** can help you to overcome that problem. It provides a chronological listing of every boundary change that has occurred in the history of Kentucky.

Atlas of Historical County Boundaries: http://publications.newberry.org/ahcbp/documents/KY_Consolidated _Chronology.htm#Consolidated_Chronology

Name Changes: Surname changes, variations, and misspellings can complicate genealogical research. It is important to check all spelling variations. Soundex, a program that indexes names by sound, is a useful first step, but you can't rely on it completely as some name variations result in different Soundex codes. The surnames could be different, but the first name may be different too. You can also find records filed under initials, middle names, and nicknames as well, so you will need to **get creative with surname variations** and spellings in order to cover all the possibilities. For help with surname variations read our instructional article on **How to Use Soundex**.

get creative with surname variations: http://obituarieshelp.org/blog/?p=634

How to Use Soundex: http://obituarieshelp.org/blog/?p=505

Kentucky Genealogical Organizations and Archives

Genealogical resources include not only records, but the organizations that house them, or can direct you to them. These institutions include: *Archives, Libraries, Genealogical Societies, Family History Centers, Universities, Churches, and Museums.*

Following are links to their websites, their physical addresses, and a summary of the records you can find there.

Department for Libraries and Archives – state and local government records including marriage records, deed books, will books, census and military records, circuit and appellate court case files, and records from additional state agencies, including the Governor's Office

Public Records Division
300 Coffee Tree Road
Frankfort, KY 40601
Toll Free Phone: 800-928-7000
Tel: 502-564-8300
Fax: 502-564-5773

Department for Libraries and Archives:
http://kdla.ky.gov/Pages/default.aspx

National Archives Southeast Region (Atlanta) - census records, land records, military records, passenger lists, immigration and naturalization records, Native and African American records

5780 Jonesboro Road
Morrow, Georgia 30260
Tel: 770-968-2100
Fax: 770-968-2547
E-mail: atlanta.archives@nara.gov

National Archives Southeast Region (Atlanta):
http://www.archives.gov/southeast/index.html

Margaret I. King Library - county, state, and federal records, church records, genealogical collections, historical manuscript collections, county and local histories,

Department of Special Collections and Archives
University of Kentucky
179 Funkhouser Dr.
Lexington, KY 40506-0039
Tel: 859-257-8611
Fax: 859-257-6311

Margaret I. King Library:
http://www.uky.edu/Libraries/lib.php?lib_id=13

Western Kentucky University Library - significant genealogical records, church histories, and biographies

1906 College Heights Blvd., #11067
Bowling Green, KY. 42101-1067
Tel: (270) 745-6125.
Fax: (270) 745-6422
E-Mail library.web@wku.edu

Western Kentucky University Library:
http://www.wku.edu/library

Lexington Public Library (Kentucky Room) - secondary sources on state and local history and genealogy, family histories, census indexes, and some census microfilm

140 East Main Street
Lexington, KY 40507
Tel: 859-231-5520

Lexington Public Library: http://www.lexpublib.org/

Kentucky Genealogical and Historical Societies

Genealogical and historical societies have access to extensive catalogues of genealogical data. They are also able to offer expert guidance for genealogical researchers. Many members are professional genealogists who are most willing to share their expertise in finding ancestors.

Kentucky Historical Society - books, manuscripts, photographs, oral histories, microfilm, and other genealogical resources

100 W. Broadway
Frankfort, KY 40601
Tel: 502-564-1792

Kentucky Historical Society: http://history.ky.gov/research-genealogy/

Kentucky Genealogical Society – county records, school records, family histories, cemetery records and other genealogical resources

PO Box 153
Frankfort, KY 40602

Kentucky Genealogical Society: http://www.kygs.org/

The African-American Genealogy Group of Kentucky – miscellaneous African American genealogy resources

P.O. Box 1211
Frankfort, KY 40602
Tel: 502.422.4457
Email: aaggky@yahoo.com

The African-American Genealogy Group of Kentucky: http://www.aaggky.org/

Additional Kentucky Genealogical Resources

Kentucky Mailing Lists

Mailing lists are internet based facilities that use email to distribute a single message to all who subscribe to it. When information on a particular surname, new records, or any other important genealogy information related to the mailing list topic becomes available, the subscribers are alerted to it. Joining a mailing list is an excellent way to stay up to date on Kentucky genealogy research topics. Rootsweb have an extensive listing of **Kentucky Mailing Lists** on a variety of topics.

Kentucky Mailing Lists:
http://lists.rootsweb.ancestry.com/index/usa/KY/misc.html

Kentucky Message Boards

A message board is another internet based facility where people can post questions about a specific genealogy topic and have it answered by other genealogists. If you have questions about a surname, record type, or research topic, you can post your question and other researchers and genealogists will help you with the answer. Be sure to check back regularly, as the answers are not emailed to you. The message boards at the **Kentucky Genealogy Forum** are completely free to use.

Kentucky Genealogy Forum: http://genforum.genealogy.com/ky/

Kentucky Newspapers and Periodicals

Many genealogy periodicals and historical newspapers contain reprinted copies of family genealogies, transcripts of family Bible records, information about local records and archives, census indexes, church records, queries, land records, obituaries, court records, cemetery records, and wills. The following sites have historical Kentucky newspapers and periodicals that you can search online or on-site.

Lexington Public Library - newspapers and periodicals of Frankfort, Ky., 1795-1945.

140 East Main Street
Lexington, KY 40507
Telephone: 859-231-5520

Lexington Public Library: http://www.lexpublib.org/

Kenton County Public Library - newspaper index for the years 1835 to 1931 and 1984 to the present

502 Scott Blvd
Covington, KY 41011
Telephone: 859-962-4070

Kenton County Public Library: http://www.kenton.lib.ky.us

GenealogyBank.com – free searchable database of Kentucky newspaper archives, 1794-1922

GenealogyBank.com:
http://www.genealogybank.com/gbnk/newspapers/explore/USA/Kentucky/

Library of Congress Digital Newspaper Directory – free searchable database of historical U.S. newspapers dating from 1690-present

Library of Congress Digital Newspaper Directory: http://chroniclingamerica.loc.gov/search/titles/

The Online Books Page – links to historical books and periodicals available for viewing online, dating from mid-16th century

The Online Books Page: http://onlinebooks.library.upenn.edu/webbin/book//browse?type=lcs ubc&key=Kentucky%20--%20History%20--%20Periodicals

NewspaperArchive.com – largest online database of historical newspapers in the world.

NewspaperArchive.com: http://newspaperarchive.com/

Historical Kentucky Maps and Gazetteers

Maps are an integral part of genealogical research. They help us to locate landmarks, towns, cities, parishes, states, provinces, waterways and roads and streets. They also help us to determine when and where boundary changes might have taken place, and give us a visualization of the area we're researching in.

For locating place names, a gazetteer is the best possible resource for any genealogist. Gazetteers are also sometimes called "place name dictionaries", and can help you to locate the area in which you need to conduct research. Below are links to the maps and gazetteers for research in Kentucky.

Peabody GNIS Service – Kentucky:
http://peabody.research.yale.edu/cgi-bin/Query.GNIS?ST=Kentucky&SU=1

Color Landform Atlas – Kentucky:
http://fermi.jhuapl.edu/states/ky_0.html

1985 U.S. Atlas: http://www.livgenmi.com/1895/KY/

Kentucky Hometown Locator:
http://kentucky.hometownlocator.com/

Kentucky City Directories

.

City directories are similar to telephone directories in that they list the residents of a particular area. The difference though is what is important to genealogists, and that is they pre-date telephone directories. You can find an ancestor's information such as their street address, place of employment, occupation, or the name of their spouse. A one-stop-shop for finding city directories in Kentucky is the **Kentucky Online Historical Directories** which contains a listing of every available historical directory related to Kentucky.

Kentucky Online Historical Directories:
https://sites.google.com/site/onlinedirectorysite/Home/usa/ky

Kentucky Genealogical Records

Birth, Death, Marriage and Divorce Records – Also known as vital records, birth, death, and marriage certificates are the most basic, yet most important records attached to your ancestor. The reason for their importance is that they not only place your ancestor in a specific place at a definite time, but potentially connect the individual to other relatives. Below is a list of repositories and websites where you can find Kentucky vital records

Kentucky's Vital Statistics Law provided for and the legalization and the registration of births and deaths. The **Kentucky Office of Vital Statistics** has birth records dating from 1911, and delayed records of births for those born before 1911. Copies can be ordered by contacting:

Office of Vital Statistics
275 E. Main St., 1E-A
Frankfort, KY 40621
Tel: (502) 564-4212

Kentucky Office of Vital Statistics: http://chfs.ky.gov/dph/vital/

The **University of Kentucky** has the following indexes that can be searched online:

1. KENTUCKY DEATH INDEX FOR 1911-1986
2. KENTUCKY MARRIAGE INDEX FOR 1973-1993
3. KENTUCKY DEATH INDEX FOR 1987-1992
4. KENTUCKY DIVORCE INDEX FOR 1973-1993

University of Kentucky: http://ukcc.uky.edu/vitalrec/

Family Search has the following indexes that are searchable online:

1. **Kentucky Births and Christenings, 1839-1960**
2. **Kentucky Marriages, 1785-1979**
3. **Kentucky, County Marriages, 1797-1954**
4. **Kentucky, Death Records, 1911-1955**
5. **Kentucky Deaths and Burials, 1843-1970**

Kentucky Births and Christenings, 1839-1960:
https://familysearch.org/search/collection/1674843

Kentucky Marriages, 1785-1979:
https://familysearch.org/search/collection/1674849

Kentucky, County Marriages, 1797-1954:
https://familysearch.org/search/collection/1804888

Kentucky, Death Records, 1911-1955:
https://familysearch.org/search/collection/1417491

Kentucky Deaths and Burials, 1843-1970:
https://familysearch.org/search/collection/1674848

Other Marriage and Divorce Records Sources

Central registration of marriages and divorces began in Kentucky in June 1958. The **Office of Vital Statistics** has records of marriages or divorces after 1958. Marriage certificates prior to June 1958 can be found at **Kentucky County Clerk's Offices** in the county where the marriage license was issued.

Office of Vital Statistics: http://chfs.ky.gov/dph/vital/

Kentucky County Clerk's Offices:
http://elect.ky.gov/contactcountyclerks/pages/default.aspx

Census Reports

Census records are among the most important genealogical documents for placing your ancestor in a particular place at a specific time. Like BDM records, they can also lead you to other ancestors, particularly those who were living under the authority of the head of household.
Census records:
http://obituarieshelp.org/utilizing_census_returns.html

Federal census records for Kentucky exist from 1790 through 1930, and can be found in the following repositories:

Lexington Public Library – Kentucky census records from 1790-1930

140 East Main Street
Lexington, KY 40507
Telephone: 859-231-5520

Lexington Public Library: http://www.lexpublib.org/page/ky-census-records-1790-1930

The **Free Census Project** has transcribed many Kentucky indexes and new material is added daily

Free Census Project: http://usgwcensus.org/cenfiles/ky.htm

Access Genealogy – Kentucky county census records from 1790

Access Genealogy:
http://www.accessgenealogy.com/census/kentucky-census-records.htm

African American Census Schedules Online – slave schedules, mortality schedules, slave-owners census

African American Census Schedules Online:
http://www.afrigeneas.com/aacensus/ga/

Native Americans in Census Records (US National Archives)

Native Americans in Census Records:
http://www.archives.gov/research/census/native-americans/

Kentucky Church Records

Church and synagogue records are a valuable resource, especially for baptisms, marriages, and burials that took place before 1900. You will need to at least have an idea of your ancestor's religious denomination, and in most cases you will have to visit a brick and mortar establishment to view them.

Most church records are kept by the individual church, although in some denominations, records are placed in a regional archive or maintained at the diocesan level. Local Historical Societies are sometimes the repository for the state's older church records. Below are links archives that maintain church records, as well as a few databases that can be viewed online.

The **Family History Library** contains many church records from a variety of denominations on microfilm.

Family History Library:
http://familysearch.org/learn/wiki/en/Family_History_Library

The **Kentucky Digital Library** has a massive directory of Church records that can be found at the University of Kentucky. Records date from the early 19th century to modern times and include every denomination that practices in the state.

Kentucky Digital Library:
http://kdl.kyvl.org/?commit=search&f%5Bformat%5D%5B%5D=collections&page=1&q=church+records&search_field=all_fields

Central Repositories for Denominational Records

Most of the records of individual denominations are kept in central repositories. Below is a list of the major congregational archives for Kentucky with links to their websites, physical addresses, and contact information.

Southern Baptist

Southern Baptist Theological Seminary
Boyce Centennial Library
2825 Lexington Road
Louisville, KY 40280
E-mail: boyce@sbts.edu

Southern Baptist Theological Seminary: http://library.sbts.edu/

Methodist

Kentucky Annual Conference
2000 Warrington Way
Browenton Building, Suite 28
Louisville, KY 40222-340
Telephone: 1-502-425-388
Fax: 1-502-426-5181

Kentucky Annual Conference: http://www.kyumc.org/

Redbird Mission Conference
6 Queendale Center
Beverley, KY 40913
Telephone: 1-606-598-5915
Fax: 1-606-598-6405

Redbird Mission Conference: http://rbmission.org/

Early **Mormon Church** records for Kentucky can be found on film located at the LDS Family History Library in Salt Lake City and can be searched via the **Family History Library Catalog**

Family History Library Catalog:
https://familysearch.org/eng/Library/FHLC/frameset_fhlc.asp

Roman Catholic

Diocese of Covington
Office of the Archive
P.O. Box 18548
Erlanger, KY 41018-0548
Telephone: 1-606-283-6210
Fax: 1-606-283-6334

Diocese of Covington: http://www.covingtondiocese.org/

Diocese of Lexington
1310 West Main Street
Lexington, KY 40508-2040
Telephone: 1-606-253-1993

Diocese of Lexington: http://www.cdlex.org/

Archdiocese of Louisville
212 East College Street
Louisville, KY 40203
Telephone: 1-502-585-3291

Archdiocese of Louisville: http://www.archlou.org/

Diocese of Owensboro
Catholic Pastoral Center
600 Locust Street
Owensboro, KY 42301
Telephone: 1-502-683-1545

Diocese of Owensboro: http://www.rcdok.org/

Presbyterian

Presbyterian Historical Society
318 Georgia Terrace
Montreat, NC 38757
Telephone: 1-828-669-7061
Fax: 1-828-669-5369

Mailing address:

Presbyterian Historical Society
P.O. Box 849
Montreat, NC 38757

Presbyterian Historical Society: http://www.phcmontreat.org/

Kentucky Military Records

More than 40 million Americans have participated in some time of war service since America was colonized. The chance of finding your ancestor amongst those records is exceptionally high. Military records can even reveal individuals who never actually served, such as those who registered for the two World Wars but were never called to duty.

Below are a number of links to websites and archives that contain Kentucky military records.

Kentucky Department for Libraries and Archives – Militia Muster Rolls for Indian Wars (1791-1811), War of 1812 Adjutant General's Report, Mexican War Adjutant General's Report, Civil War Service Records, Civil War Adjutant General's Report, Confederate Pension Applications, Spanish American War Adjutant General's Report, World War I Draft Registration Cards, World War I Service Cards, Kentucky Veteran's Bonus Applications, Kentucky State/National Guard 1875-1940

Public Records Division
300 Coffee Tree Road
Frankfort, KY 40601
Toll Free Phone: 800-928-7000
Tel: 502-564-8300
Fax: 502-564-5773

Department for Libraries and Archives:
http://kdla.ky.gov/Pages/default.aspx

U.S. National Archives – WWI Draft registration cards, casualties lists, WWI and WWII service records, Korean War records, Vietnam War records, Civil War and Spanish-American War records, and casualties lists.

U.S. National Archives:
http://www.archives.gov/research/military/veterans/online.html

US Department of Veterans Affairs Nationwide Gravesite Locator – includes information on veterans and their family members buried in veterans and military cemeteries having a government grave marker.

US Department of Veterans Affairs Nationwide Gravesite Locator: http://gravelocator.cem.va.gov/

United States Index to Indian Wars Pension Files, 1892-1926 – military pension records of soldiers who fought in the Indian Wars between 1817 and 1898

United States Index to Indian Wars Pension Files, 1892-1926: https://familysearch.org/search/collection/1979427

United States Registers of Enlistments in the U.S. Army, 1798-1914 - index of men who enlisted in the United States Army, 1798-1914.

United States Registers of Enlistments in the U.S. Army, 1798-1914: https://familysearch.org/search/collection/1880762

United States Mexican War Pension Index, 1887-1926 - index to Mexican War pension files for service between 1846 and 1848

United States Mexican War Pension Index, 1887-1926: https://familysearch.org/search/collection/1979390

Civil War Soldiers Service Records - Service records for both Union and Confederate soldiers indexed by soldier's name, rank, and unit.

Civil War Soldier Service Records: http://go.fold3.com/civilwar_records/

Kentucky Cemetery Records

As convenient as it is to search cemetery records online, keep in mind that there are a few disadvantages over visiting a cemetery in person. They are:

- Tombstone information is not always accurately transcribed
- The arrangement of the graves in a cemetery can be crucial as family members are often buried next to each other or in the same grave. This arrangement is not always preserved in the alphabetical indexes that are found online.

With that information in mind, the following websites have databases that can be searched online for Kentucky Cemetery records.

Kentucky Tombstone Transcription Project - death and burial records

Kentucky Tombstone Transcription Project:
http://www.usgwtombstones.org/kentucky/kentucky.html

African American Cemeteries Online – African American, slave, and Native American cemetery records

African American Cemeteries Online:
http://africanamericancemeteries.com/ar/

Access Genealogy – huge database of Kentucky cemetery record transcriptions

Access Genealogy:
http://www.accessgenealogy.com/cemetery/kentucky-cemetery-records.htm

Find a Grave – over 100 million grave records can be searched on this site. Search can be conducted by name, location, or cemetery name.

Find a Grave: http://www.findagrave.com/

Interment.net - A free online database containing approximately 4 million cemetery records from around the world.

Interment.net: http://www.interment.net/

Billion Graves – as the name implies, you can search a billion records including headstone photos, transcriptions, cemetery records, and grave locations.

Billion Graves:
http://billiongraves.com/pages/search/index.php#cemetery

Kentucky Obituaries

Obituaries can reveal a wealth about our ancestor and other relatives. You can search our **Kentucky Newspaper Obituaries Listings** from hundreds of Kentucky newspapers online for free.

Kentucky Newspaper Obituaries Listings:
http://obituarieshelp.org/kentucky_newspaper_obituaries.html

Kentucky Wills and Probate Records

The documents found in a probate packet may include a complete inventory of a person's estate, newspaper entries, witness testimony, a copy of a will, list of debtors and creditors, names of executors or trustees, names of heirs. They can not only tell you about the ancestor you're currently researching, but lead to other ancestors.

Most of these records must be accessed at a county court or clerk's office, but some can be found online as well. You can obtain copies of the original probate records by writing to the county clerk.

Kentucky probate records are kept by the **County Clerks**, but copies of probate records can be found at:

Kentucky Historical Society

100 W. Broadway
Frankfort, KY 40601
Tel: 502-564-1792

Kentucky Historical Society: http://history.ky.gov/research-genealogy/

Department for Libraries and Archives

Public Records Division
300 Coffee Tree Road
Frankfort, KY 40601
Toll Free Phone: 800-928-7000
Tel: 502-564-8300
Fax: 502-564-5773

Department for Libraries and Archives:
http://kdla.ky.gov/Pages/default.aspx

County Clerks:
http://elect.ky.gov/contactcountyclerks/pages/default.aspx

Family Search has an online index - **Kentucky Probate Records, 1727-1990**

Kentucky Probate Records, 1727-1990:
https://familysearch.org/search/collection/1875188

Kentucky Immigration and Naturalization Records

The naturalization process generated many types of records, including petitions, declarations of intention, and oaths of allegiance. These records can provide family historians with information such as a person's birth date and place of birth, immigration year, marital status, spouse information, occupation, witnesses' names and addresses, and more.

Most overseas immigrants came to Kentucky through east coast ports such as New York and Philadelphia, and then traveled by railway to Kentucky. Earlier immigrants landed at New Orleans and then traveled by steamboats upriver to Kentucky. The **U.S. National Archives** has passenger lists or indexes of American ports for 1820 to 1940, as well as immigration and naturalization records for the entire United States. These records can also be accessed at the **National Archives Regional Branch in Atlanta**

US National Archives:
http://www.archives.gov/research/immigration/passenger-arrival.html

National Archives Regional Branch in Atlanta:
http://www.archives.gov/atlanta/

Kentucky Native American Records

Laurel County Public Library – Native American census rolls, mostly Cherokee

Laurel County Public Library
120 College Park Drive
London, KY 40741
Phone: (606) 864-5759

Laurel County Public Library:
http://www.laurellibrary.org/kentuckyroom/

Access Genealogy – Kentucky Native American census records, tribal histories, and much more

Access Genealogy:
http://www.accessgenealogy.com/native/kentucky-indian-tribes.htm

Records of the Bureau of Indian Affairs (BIA)

Records of the Bureau of Indian Affairs (BIA):
http://www.archives.gov/research/guide-fed-records/groups/075.html

American Indians Records Repository - records dating from the 1700s including trust, education and other historic Indian Affairs records

American Indian Records Repository
Meritex Enterprises
17501 West 98th Street
Lenexa, KS 66219
Phone: 913-888-0601

American Indians Records Repository:
http://www.doi.gov/ost/records_mgmt/american-indian-records-repository.cfm

Missing Matriarchs – Resources for Researching Female Kaentucky Ancestors

Looking for female ancestors requires an adjustment of how we view traditional records sources. A woman's identity was often under that of her husband, and often individual records for them can be difficult to locate. The following resources are effective in locating female ancestors in Kentucky where traditional records may not reveal them.

Marriage and Divorce Records

Marriages have been recorded in county records since the creation date of individual counties. State-wide registration began in 1958. The first divorces were granted by the Kentucky State Legislature, though from 1849-1959, county courts held jurisdiction. Additional records to those listed previously which may be of assistance are:

- Fayette County Clerk marriage bonds, 1803-1898, and minister marriage returns, 1795-1851 (film 0009014 ff.) at the **William T. Young Library**, University of Kentucky, Lexington
- Floyd County Circuit Court order books, 1808-1934 (film 1843752 ff.) at the Floyd County Courthouse in Prestonburg
- Lincoln County Clerk of the County Court marriage records, 1781-1961 (film 1904116 ff.) at the Lincoln County Courthouse in Stanford

William T. Young Library: http://libraries.uky.edu/WTYL

Bibliographies

- *Kentucky Quilts and Their Makers,* Mary Washington Clark (University Press of Kentucky, 1993)
- *Appalachian Women: An Annotated Bibliography,* Sidney S. Farr (Robert Clarke & Co. 1870)
- *Coal Miners Wives: Portraits of Endurance,* Carol Giesen (University of Kentucky Press, 1995)

- *Kentucky Families: A Bibliographic Listing,* Donald M. Hehir (Heritage Books, 1993)
- *Women in Kentucky,* Helen Deiss Irvin (University of Kentucky Press, 1979)

Selected Resources for Kentucky Women's History

Women's Coalition of Kentucky
Blazer Library
Kentucky State University
East Main Street
Frankfort, KY 40601

University of Kentucky Libraries
Euclid Avenue and Rose St.
Lexington, KY 40601

Camden-Carroll Library
Morehead State University
150 University Blvd
Morehead, KY 40351

Common Kentucky Surnames

The following surnames are among the most common in Kentucky and are also being currently researched by other genealogists. If you find your surname here, there is a chance that some research has already been performed on your ancestor.

Abell, Adams, Alexander, Allen), Anderson, Antle, Armstrong, Banks, Barnett, Barrett, Bashaw, Batterton, Beauchamp, Bell, Berry, Bird, Black, Blue, Bozarth, Bradley, Branch, Breckenridge, Bridges, Brown, Bryan, Bullard, Burch, Burtle, Calvert, Campbell, Cantrall, Cartmell, Cartwright, Cassity, Clayton, Cloyd, Constant, Courtney, Crafton, Craig, Crowder, Darneille, Davies, Davis, Dawson, Delay, Dick, Dickerson, Dodds, Dohoney, Dozier, Drennan, Duncan, Earnest, Easley, Eaton, Edwards, Elliott, Ellis, Enyart, Etherington, Etherton, Ezell, Fletcher, Flick, For, Forrest, Foster, Fullinwider, Gaines, Gibson, Goff, Graham, Graves, Greening, Greenslate, Hammons, Hampton, Harrison, Hays, Hickman, Higgins, Highsmith, Hinchee, Hubbard, Jacobs, James, Johnson, Jones, Kendall, Kennedy, Lagow, Lanterman, Laswell, Laughlin, Leeper, Lewis, Lightfoot, Lindsay, Lloyd, Lyon, Mann, Martin, Maxcy, McBride, McCoy, McCune, McGinnis, McGowan, McIlvain, Merriman, Miller, Moffitt, Moore, Morgan, Nation, Nuttall, Organ, Peddecord, Pickrell, Price, Rankin, Ray, Raybourn, Rich, Ridgeway, Riley, Robinson, Rogers, Schultz, Scott, Sexton, Shutt, Smith, Summers, Taylor, Thompson, Threllkild, Tolley, Tomlinson, Turpin, Underwood, Utterbach, Vigal, Viney, Walker, Wallace, Walls, Watkins, Watts, Webb, Weger, White, Whitesides, Williams, Willis, Wills), Wilmot, Wilson, Withrow, Woodruff, Workman, Wright), Wyckoff, Yancey, Yates, Yoakum), York, Young), Younger, Zinn

About the Author

Gary L. Morris worked from 2009 to 2014 as a professional researcher for a major player in the genealogy field. After tracing his family lineage back to 1683, he has decided to publish these helpful guides to share the valuable information he has discovered during his career to help others trace their family lineages. An avid genealogist himself, he hopes you will find this guide factual, thorough, helpful, and most of all, effective in helping you to find your family members.

www.ingramcontent.com/pod-product-compliance
Lightning Source LLC
Chambersburg PA
CBHW072021290526
45787CB00013B/1604